THE ILLUSTRATED
TEXAS
DICTIONARY
of the
ENGLISH LANGUAGE
VOLUME TWO

by Jim Everhart

With 47 photographs of the author

by Bert Brandt

CLIFF'S NOTES, INC. · BOX 428, LINCOLN, NEBRASKA 68501

all—petroleum. "They found *all* on mah land!"

doll—the process used to operate a telephone. "Why that's a terrible mess of numbers to *doll* for a long distance call!"

wunst—one time and no more.
"Call me that again, *wunst* more."

pawn—on top of; above. "Ah'm not gonna tell yew again to get off from *pawn* that table."

banes—large, smooth kidney-shaped, edible seeds. "Ah could eat mah weight in pinto *banes*."

slave—the part of a garment covering an arm only. "Are yew sayin' mah left *slave* is shorter than mah riot?"

wuf—a large, doglike
carnivorous mammal.
"Who's afraid of the
beg, bad *wuf*. . . ?"

whalebarah—a small vehicle with handles and one wheel for conveying small loads. "Be careful! Don't let that *whalebarah* tump over."

node—past tense of "know." "Ah *node* ah shouldn't of bent over in these ol' britches."

paypal — a body of persons. "Where'd all them *paypal* come from?"

barred — (past tense), to receive with the expressed intention of returning the same. "Who *barred* mah hat an' didn't brang it back?"

kaint—contraction for "can not."
"Stop it! Yew *kaint* do it that way."

lane—to incline or bend from a vertical position. "All she did was *lane* her had on mah shoulder."

sep—to omit or bar. "Everybody can go in *sep* yew!"

coarse—a body of dancers and singers who execute special numbers. "Yore one of them *coarse* girls ain't yew?"

stars—a flight of steps. "If yawl thank ah'm gonna walk up all them *stars* yawl are crazy."

rueing—state of being destroyed, wrecked, etc. "Yawl are drivin' me to rack and *rueing!*"

lags—the limbs of man used for supporting the body. "That gal's *lags* look lack a stockin' full of rocks."

sacks—the character of being male or female. "Well, there's the male *sacks* an' then there's the female *sacks*. . . ."

are—sixty minutes. "Ah'll meet yew there in about a *are*."

grain—a color. "He's jes *grain* with envy."

quahr—an organized company of singers. "Yes, mam, ah sang in the church *quahr* every Sunday."

lon—a large, carnivorous mammal of the cat family. "Yew tellin' me them Romans thowed the Christians to the *lons!*"

spell—to fall down.
"Oooooeeeee! He sure took a nasty *spell*."

bean—a living person.
"He's one of the finest
human *beans* ah ever met."

ast—the past tense of the word, "ask."
"Who *ast* yew!"

foured—the part of the face above the eyes. "The sweat's jes pourin' often mah *foured*."

stale—to take and carry away feloniously. "Thou shalt not *stale*. . . ."

kwat—free from noise or disturbance. "Be *kwat*; yawl are makin' too much noise!"

tearse—a courtyard usually planted with trees and shrubs. "That thang yew call a *tearse* ain't nuthin' but a lil ol' patio."

favor—to run a temperature. "Ah thank ah got a *favor*."

sense—from a definite past time until now. "Ah kaint even doll the telephone *sense* ah hurt mah fanger."

warsh—to cleanse by rubbing or scrubbing in water. "Pardon me, ah'm gonna *warsh* mah hands."

wrench—to wash lightly with water. "Can ah hep yew *wrench* off them dishes?"

bear—a fermented liquor brewed from malt and flavored with hops. "All ah had was one bottle of *bear*."

tempetour—the degree of hotness or coldness. "Boy, the *tempetour* must be about a hundred today."

libel—apt or likely to. "Don't never try to walk lack this or yore *libel* to bust a lag."

arn — a silver-white metallic element. "Mah muscle is as strong as *arn*."

mihyun—the number immediately following 999,999. "If ah told yew wunst ah told yew a *mihyun* toms."

error—the missile used with a bow. "Ah shot a *error* into the air, an' where it fell ah node not where. . . ."

par — exerted energy, force, or might. "If yew can do that, more *par* to yew."

sar—having an acid or tart taste. "Boy, is that lemon ever *sar!*"

nekked — having on no clothes, nude. ". . . and there he was *nekked* as a jaybird."

tuther—being the one of two (or more). "Yew kaint have both; take one or the *tuther*."

card—a person who lacks courage. "Ah'm callin' yew a yella-bellied *card!*"

Ainglish—the language spoken in the United Kingdom and the United States. "What's the matter with yew, kaint yew understand the kang's *Ainglish?*"